HERALD BIBLICAL BOOKLETS
Robert J. Karris O.F.M., General Editor

KNOWING CHRIST THROUGH MARK'S GOSPEL

by PHILIP VAN LINDEN C.M.

FRANCISCAN HERALD PRESS
1434 West 51st Street • Chicago, Illinois 60609

Knowing Christ Through Mark's Gospel, by Philip Van Linden, C.M. Copyright © 1977 by Franciscan Herald Press, 1434 West 51st Street, Chicago, Illinois 60609. Made in the United States of America.

Library of Congress Cataloging in Publication Data

Van Linden, Philip.
   Knowing Christ through Mark's gospel.

   (Herald Biblical booklet series)
   Bibliography: p.
   1. Bible. N.T. Mark–Study–Text-books. I. Title.
BS2585.5.V36   226'.3'007   76-21787
ISBN 0-8199-0727-8

Nihil Obstat:
   John A. Grindel, C.M.
   Censor Deputatus

Imprimatur:
   Timothy Cardinal Manning
   Archbishop of Los Angeles

March 30, 1976

> "The Nihil Obstat and the Imprimatur are official declarations that a book or pamphlet is free of doctrinal or moral error. No implication is contained therein that those who have granted the Nihil Obstat and Imprimatur agree with the contents, opinions or statements expressed."

CONTENTS

PREFACE..............................5

INTRODUCTION......................7

1. A FIVE-STEP APPROACH
                TO THE BIBLE........11

2. GETTING IN TOUCH WITH
            THE GOSPEL OF MARK.......24

3. THE LEPER AND THE
        MISUNDERSTOOD MESSIAH....39

4. WHO DO YOU SAY THAT I AM?......51

5. FOLLOWING JESUS ALL THE
                WAY --- TODAY 61

CONCLUSION 72

FOR FURTHER STUDY 73

LEADER'S GUIDE....................77

PREFACE

THIS BOOKLET HAS BEEN PREPARED for the use of those who are serious about meeting God in His Word, either individually or in a study group. What I have written can be properly read and understood only with the prayerful reading and involvement with God's own Word. My sincere thanks go to those many serious Catholics who have urged me to prepare this study guide. I am also most grateful to Fathers Bernard Quinn, C.M. and Richard Ryan, and to Mrs. Josephine Dober who took the time and care to help me with this booklet.

> Philip Van Linden, C.M.
> January, 1976
> St. John's Seminary
> Camarillo, California

INTRODUCTION

This booklet was conceived in my work with Catholic adults who, for years, have urged me to put together a Scripture study guide for them. Seminary students, fellow priests, sisters, lay friends, members of parish study groups, and participants in the Catholic Charismatic movement and Marriage Encounter--all of them have expressed the same need: "We need help and guidance in reading and interpreting the Bible as Catholics. Other Christian denominations and Jews seem to know more about the Bible than we do. Long ago they developed means to help their people hear God speak in His Word. We look to the Church for proper leadership and assistance."

This request has not been unheard. Nor has the Church only recently been aware of the need. In 1893 Pope Leo XIII "cherished the desire to give an impulse to the noble science of Holy Scripture, and to impart to Scripture study a direction suitable to the needs of the present day" (*Providentissimus Deus*, in *Rome and the Study of Scripture* (Abbey Press, 1964), p.2). He quoted St. Jerome: "to be ignorant of the Scripture is not to know Christ." Pius X, in 1907, proclaimed that proper study of Scripture was a "most useful undertaking, as well as most suited to the times" seeing that it helps in no small way to "dissipate the idea that the Church is opposed to or in any way impedes the reading of the Scriptures" (Quote from Letter to Cardinal Casetta, found in *Rome and the Study of Scripture*, p. 96). The Fathers of the Second Vatican Council strongly repeated and developed the monumental message of Pius XII who in 1943 gave modern Scripture study its greatest impulse in *Divino Afflante Spiritus*. The Council Fathers said:

> The Church has always regarded, and continues to regard the Scriptures, taken together with sacred Tradition, as the supreme rule of her faith... In the sacred books the Father who is in heaven comes lovingly to meet his Children, and talks with them. And such is the force and power of the Word of God that it can serve the Church as her support and vigor, and the Children of the Church as strength for their faith, food for the soul, and a pure and lasting fount of spiritual life (Par. 21 of Divine Revelation, *Vatican Council II*, p.762).

In the past 30 years many excellent Roman Catholic scholars have produced competent popularizations of more technical biblical research. However, the Good News is still just beginning to filter down to the average Catholic. This booklet is an attempt to continue the process encouraged by Popes and Council and to further the work begun by competent scholars. Its aim is to help Catholics come into direct and enriching contact with God and His Word.

THIS BOOKLET *IS NOT* a simplistic, superficial introduction about the Bible. It is not a study on some particular theme of the Bible, nor is it a thesis for other scholars to read. It does not attempt to treat every biblical question.

THIS BOOKLET *IS* MEANT TO BE a solid, simple, stimulating guide to a proper understanding of God's Word as found in the first gospel, the gospel of Mark. It is meant to bring Catholics into deep, experiential contact with Jesus as one inspired author presents him to us. The aim of his work is to instill the confidence that each of us is capable of approaching the Bible in a professional and personal way, the only valid approach which can truly be called prayerful.

TO DERIVE THE MOST from this guide it is necessary that each person using it be hungry for God's Word. The methodology which shall be suggested will help satisfy that hunger. It will also be helpful if each person has a good translation of the Bible, like the *New American Bible*. Finally, it is vital that each person be committed to a patient participation in the assignments suggested in the following pages, with both mind and heart open to God. Such a professional and personal approach is the only way to be prayerful in responding to his challenging Word.

THIS IS A STUDY GUIDE; thus review or discussion questions follow each chapter. The first two chapters are meant to familiarize the reader with proper Bible study and with Mark's gospel by providing sufficient background information. Chapters three to five challenge the student of God's Word to work with the Bible texts directly. A leader's guide is provided to help in the discussions and projects which might arise from the use of the booklet.

A DREAM. "The Church has always venerated the divine Scriptures just as she venerated the Body of the Lord, in so far as she never ceases, particularly in the sacred Liturgy, to partake of the bread of life and to offer it to the faithful from the one table of the Word of God and the Body of Christ. . . . Access to sacred Scripture ought to be open wide to the Christian faithful" (Par. 21 of Divine Revelation, *Vatican Council II*, p.762). This dream of the Council Fathers is the dream of many Catholics. May it one day become a reality.

1. A FIVE-STEP APPROACH TO THE BIBLE

WHERE DO WE START? Many people become frustrated and bewildered when they begin reading the Bible. In this first chapter I would like you to become acquainted and involved with the basic principles of Bible study. I present them to you in *Five Steps*, and then conclude with a summary explanation and a graphic presentation in order to make these important principles clear. So we start. . . with step one.

STEP ONE: BACKGROUND INFORMATION

YOU'RE DRIVING ALONG IN YOUR CAR. You switch on the radio to hear the last lilting lines of a pleasant sounding song:

> Follow me where I go, who I am, and who I know,
>
> Make it part of you to be a part of me.

You either like the song or you don't. If you do, you might listen for it again. You might hum along with it, or whistle it later in the day. It has left a gentle, but hardly deep, impression on you.

Then you meet someone who is a Mary Travers fanatic like me. I tell you that this "Follow Me" is the song that brought Mary back as a performing artist. You're wondering who Mary

Travers is anyway. Then I tell you that she is Mary from the *Peter, Paul and Mary* group that sang "500 Miles" and "Blowing in the Wind." Remember the group? Yes, you do. You liked them. Whatever happened to them? Well, they broke up and went their separate ways. Mary is now alone and trying to re-establish herself as a singer. She still has her loyal followers. Likewise, they mean a great deal to her, and she wants to make them a part of her life once again. But she can't do it alone, so she urges them to follow her in her song.

You've learned much about the person who sang that pleasant song. The next time you hear it your mind wanders a bit. You hear much more in the words. You hear Mary singing with her whole heart. She is singing directly to real people about her very real life. The background information you received from me has helped you to appreciate her song much more.

I HOPE THIS SIMPLE EXAMPLE BRINGS OUT the value of what scholars call *historical criticism* in their effort to bring about a true appreciation of a work of art, like a painting, a song, the Bible. Background information about a performer or author helps one hear and understand what the performer or author wishes to express more completely and more richly.

GOD'S WORD IS TRULY A WORK OF ART. It was not just thrown together or dictated from heaven but is the work of special men that God chose. He chose his communicators well, for each one of the inspired writers is an artist in his own right. And the result of God's loving choice of each author is a gift of love through which he wished to communicate something special to a specific people in a particular situation. . . then, when each book was originally written; and now, when each book is read.

Consequently, as we begin our Bible Study of Mark's gospel, it will be most helpful if we ask the following questions:

WHO WAS MARK? WHEN DID HE WRITE? UNDER WHAT CIRCUMSTANCES? FOR WHOM DID HE WRITE? WHAT WAS THE OVERRIDING PURPOSE OF HIS CREATION?

We will deal with these questions in chapter two. Such an investigation will help us appreciate what God really wishes to say to us today.

STEP TWO: SEEING THE WHOLE PICTURE

HAVE YOU EVER BEEN TO A THEATER when the movie projector happened to be out of focus? In Europe people clap their hands until the projectionist adjusts the focus. In America they yell back at the projection booth behind them. The slightest touch of the focusing apparatus can distort the whole picture. Similarly, no work of literature can be enjoyed and properly understood unless it is put into its proper literary focus.

Or have you ever looked forward to seeing a movie on television which you really enjoyed in the theater? And then been totally disappointed when the most dramatic moments were interrupted by a ten-minute interlude of panty hose, drain cleaners, and the conclusive evidence that this brand of aspirin works better than other brands? In the same way, we cannot expect to enjoy God's Word, like the gospel of Mark, if we never sit down to read it from beginning to end. If we only taste it in bits and pieces, a few verses each Sunday over the course of many weeks, we can hardly expect to be personally and totally involved with the movement of the whole drama.

Hopefully then, the importance of asking the following questions *about the whole gospel* will be clear:

HOW DOES MARK'S GOSPEL BEGIN AND END? WHERE DOES THE GOSPEL REACH ITS CLIMAX? WHERE DOES THE STORY LEAD? HOW DOES HE BUILD UP THE DRAMA? IN WHAT LIGHT IS JESUS CAST? AND THE OTHER LEADING CHARACTERS? ARE THERE ANY RE-

CURRING BASIC QUESTIONS THAT MARK DEALS WITH THROUGHOUT THE WHOLE GOSPEL?

Biblical scholars refer to one phase of the critical *study of the whole gospel* as *redaction criticism* (the study of the editing done by the gospel writers). We shall be involved in this in the chapters that follow, as we seek to recognize which beliefs and attitudes seemed to Mark particularly vital in the situation in which he wrote. We shall try to see at which points in his gospel he selected and arranged his material in order to give them prominence.

STEP THREE: COMPARING LOOK-ALIKES

OFTEN WE MEET A PERSON WHO REMINDS US OF SOMEONE ELSE. He looks like the person we know, or talks or walks like him. Then, on closer observation, we find that this person is indeed very unique and very different from our former acquaintance. Likewise, the song *Follow Me* by Mary Travers has its counterpart sung by some male performer. Although they are alike, they are very different.

MARK'S GOSPEL HAS TWO LOOK-ALIKES, namely, the gospels of Matthew and Luke. These three gospels are so alike and parallel each other so often that they are called the *synoptic gospels*. They are called synoptic gospels because the various points of their agreement and divergence can be easily traced in a *synopsis*, a reference work in which the texts of the three gospels are printed in parallel columns. (The term *synoptic* is derived from the Greek word for "seeing together").

When we compare Mark, Matthew, and Luke side by side in a *synopsis*, it becomes clear that *Mark* paints his sixteen-chapter portrait of Jesus in more rapid, simple and dramatic strokes than the others. *Matthew* is more orderly and systematic in his twenty-eight chapter presentation of the same story of Jesus. *Luke*, the third author of a look-alike gospel, is the first writer to include the important ascension account and the only one to extend his twenty-four chapter gospel about Jesus by writing the Acts of the Apostles.

Such a comparison of these three similar gospels is another aspect of the *literary criticism* used by scholars to determine the actual literary relationships among the synoptic gospels. For example, it is helpful to know which gospel came first and thus became the source for the other two. Today, most scholars believe that Mark was first and that Matthew and Luke depended on him when they wrote their gospels. By our own careful comparison of portions of these gospels we can conceivably see what Mark wanted to emphasize, and how Matthew and Luke (when they differ from Mark) chose to adapt and emphasize other aspects of the same story.

> Thus we will profitably ask:
> HOW DOES MATTHEW OR LUKE DIFFER FROM MARK IN PARTICULAR SECTIONS? WHAT DOES EACH INSPIRED AUTHOR WISH TO EMPHASIZE IN THE SAME STORY? WHY DID MATTHEW OR LUKE THINK THAT MARK SHOULD BE CHANGED OR ADDED TO IN CERTAIN SECTIONS?

This sort of literary criticism or comparison is often very exciting. It can help bring an individual work (e.g. Mark's gospel) into much clearer focus. In gospel comparison we can often perceive the special mood which the author himself wished to create and express. We shall do such comparative work in the following chapters to bring the gospel of Mark into sharper focus.

STEPS FOUR AND FIVE: WHAT GOD MEANT TO SAY THEN AND NOW.

SEVERAL TIMES IN THE PRECEDING PAGES I have stressed the importance of finding out *what God really intended to say* through particular authors to a certain people at a certain time. I have emphasized this because I am convinced that we can hear *what he says to us today only* if we seriously attempt to find out what he meant to say to his original audience. The three preceding steps have been leading us to this point and to these final two steps:

WHAT DID GOD REALLY INTEND TO SAY THROUGH MARK TO HIS ORIGINAL AUDIENCE? (Step 4)
WHAT DOES HE SAY TO US TODAY?
(Step 5)

The following quotation from *The New Testament: A Guide to Its Writings* speaks directly of the importance of these final two steps:

God's Word will be heard best if we leave it in its own place, time, language and world, and if we do not immediately rush to appropriate it for ourselves. Anyone who cannot bear the remoteness and strangeness of the biblical figures and witnesses, and hence forces upon them prematurely the perspectives, ideas, and outlook of his own age---or instead runs away from his own age and pretends to be a contemporary of the Bible---rules out in advance any real encounter with the texts. By refusing to let them say what they have to say, he denies them the chance of entering into real dialogue with the kind of partner to whom they would address themselves today, namely, the person who will not only listen to the texts, but also put questions to them in return (Bornkamm, G., Fortress Press, 1973, p.29).

This quotation brings out the most important principle of valid Bible study: if we want to hear what a passage means to us today, we must first listen to God as he chose to speak through the inspired author in the first Christian century.

So many people who want to live by God's Word unknowingly violate this fundamental principle. By avoiding intelligent questioning and study (steps one through four) they remain "fundamentalistic" in their vision of and approach to the Bible. Fundamentalism is an anti-intellectual stance which refuses to take history seriously; it reads biblical (or Church) statements as if they are affected by neither time nor culture. The result of fundamentalistic Bible study is often *what people want* to hear rather than *what God wants* them to hear. As we move into the gospel of Mark it is vital that we choose to hear him as *he* chose to speak to us.

SUMMARY OF CHAPTER I

The graphic presentation (Figure 1) and

explanation which follow are meant to summarize what has already been discussed Hopefully this summary will make the key principles considered above even more clear.

Figure 1.

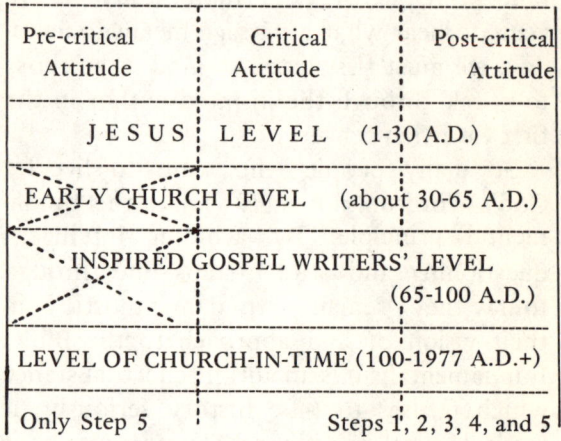

Figure 1 marks out the three possible attitudes a person can adopt in approaching and understanding God's Word, i.e. the Pre-critical, Critical, or Post-critical attitude. By "critical" here I don't mean sarcastic, destructive, faithless, or merely scientific. "To criticize", according to Webster, means "to discriminate, to separate, and to assign to each matter its proper place." Thus the critical person is one who discriminates by using

the knowledge and tools offered by biblical research, namely, the helps described in Steps 1 through 5. Please study *Figure 1* in the light of the following summary paragraphs.

THE PERSON WITH A PRE-CRITICAL ATTITUDE jumps from today to Jesus' time without paying any attention to the two periods of time when the Word was actually written down (i.e., Levels of the Early Church and Inspired Writers). Because of a fundamentalistic stance, or because of the lack of proper guidance and information, this person avoids the very levels through which the Word came to us from God. The pre-critical person *only* asks *What does God say to me today?* (Step 5)

THE PERSON WITH A CRITICAL ATTITUDE is one who asks some basic questions:

> Who is the author of this gospel, and when and why and to whom did he write? (Step 1)
> How does the inspired author organize the whole drama and why? (Step 2)
> Does a comparison of this passage in Mark's gospel with Matthew or Luke bring out any special message? (Step 3)
> What did God really intend to say to his people through Mark in 65-70 A.D.?
> (Step 4)

> What does God want me to hear, and how does he want me to respond today as I read this passage? (Step 5)

Thus, the critical person chooses to go back to what God said through Jesus, through the early Church, and through the writers he inspired by the Holy Spirit.

THE PERSON WITH A POST-CRITICAL ATTITUDE is one who is practiced and comfortable with the 5-step critical process. This person habitually applies the basic principles of understanding to a biblical text. Just as the "Mary Travers fanatic" doesn't continually ask: who is Mary Travers? what is her background? so also the post-critical reader of God's Word need not constantly go back to the basic questions. They have become a part of that person's way of reading and understanding Scripture. The post-critical person can, therefore, enjoy the truth God has led him or her to discover in his Word, as he chose to reveal it. Now is the time to "taste and see how good the Lord is", especially as he gives himself to us in his living, challenging Word.

It is the purpose of this chapter and those that follow to encourage you to become comfortable and confident in the 5-step critical process of understanding God's Word, and then to move into the post-critical stage of an enriching dialogue with God and his Word.

ASSIGNMENT AND DISCUSSION QUESTIONS FOR CHAPTER 1.

1. What is in the name MARY TRAVERS? How does some knowledge of her background help you to appreciate the song "Follow Me"?
   Please give one other example of how STEP 1 helps you to understand some work of art.
2. Please give an example of how "knowing the whole story" (STEP 2) helps you understand parts of it better.
3. What does the term "synoptic gospels" mean? Can you guess why the gospel of John is not a "synoptic gospel?"
4. What is fundamentalism?" Give an example of this.
5. What is the most important principle of a valid Bible study?
6. Please give an example of the great contrast between the way a pre-critical person appreciates some art form and the way a person in the critical or post-critical stage sees it.

(Suggested answers and aides for discussion can be found in the LEADERS' GUIDE that is appended to this booklet.)

2. GETTING IN TOUCH WITH THE GOSPEL OF MARK

MANY PEOPLE TALK ABOUT JESUS---in church on Sunday, on television and radio, in the religion section of the Sunday paper, in front rooms over coffee. It is time for Christians to *talk about* Jesus less and to *dialogue with* Him more as He communicates with us in His inspired Word. In this study, it is time to begin applying to the gospels the Five Steps described in Chapter 1. In this chapter we shall study the background information we have about Mark and his gospel (Step 1). We shall also look at the overall gospel, attempting to discover how Mark builds up the drama of Jesus' life so that it will influence his believing readers (Step 2). These pages will hopefully prepare each of us to read Mark's gospel from beginning to end as it was originally intended to be read. Such a reading will be the assignment for this chapter.

STEP ONE: BACKGROUND OF MARK'S GOSPEL. WHO WAS MARK? WHEN DID HE WRITE? UNDER WHAT CIRCUMSTANCES? FOR WHOM DID HE WRITE? WHAT WAS THE OVERRIDING PURPOSE OF HIS CREATION?

WHEN YOU OPEN YOUR NEW TESTAMENT you will see that the gospel of Matthew comes before the gospel of Mark. Although Mark was the first evangelist to write a gospel (65-70 A.D.), Matthew has occupied first place in the New Testament and in Church usage from early times. By contrast, the gospel of Mark has led a somewhat shadowy existence. Until the liturgy was renewed after the Second Vatican Council, very few excerpts from Mark were used at Mass on Sundays during the church year. Yet the importance of Mark's gospel for all Christians can hardly be overrated. Because of our former lack of exposure to Mark's gospel, it is important that we get to know as much as we can about him and his creation.

At the outset, we must realize the fact that most readers of the gospels assume that the evangelists were eyewitnesses of the events they described. Some people think that the authors knew eyewitnesses and transmitted what these eyewitnesses had seen and heard. Actually, we know very few historical details about how the gospel of Mark came to be written. Like the other gospels, it was written under the inspiration of the Spirit several decades after the death and resurrection of Jesus. An early tradition about the authorship of this gospel dates back to the second century. According to this tradition, Mark was once a travel companion of Paul and became the secretary of Peter. Most scholars today feel that this tradition has little truth to it. For such a tradition was intended to insure an indirect apostolic authority for the gospel. "This really is God's Word. After all, Mark was Paul's companion and he later heard all about Jesus from Peter, *the* apostle! So you can be sure that this gospel is the reliable truth about Jesus." Today we do not need such "proof" that this is God's Word and Truth. What the early church had to prove, we take for granted.

If "Mark," the author of the first gospel, was not Peter's disciple, who was he? It is possible to arrive at some helpful conclusions about the author of this gospel from our knowledge of the times and circumstances in which he wrote. He seems to be a zealous pastor of the newly born Christian community somewhere to the east of Palestine (Antioch?) about the time the Romans destroyed Jerusalem in 70 A.D.

Thus, he was presenting the good news about Jesus to a community of Christians who were already beginning to suffer unpopularity, persecution, and even death because of their belief in Jesus Christ as the Messiah, Son of God. In these circumstances, Mark had an OVERRIDING PURPOSE in writing: he tried to stir up in his community of believers the conviction that nothing was happening to them which lay outside of the providential love of God. The suffering they were experiencing was similar to that which Jesus experienced before them. To help his people understand what Christianity really meant, Mark gathered all the information he could find about their Lord Jesus. He then added to, adapted, and arranged the many independent stories and sayings of Jesus he had collected in order to meet the religious needs and vital questions of the people of his time.

In his attempt to explain why his fellow Christians were suffering, Mark *emphasized the cross and suffering* of Jesus in his gospel. He does this not only in the passion story at the end of the gospel, but also by adding phrases throughout the gospel that interrupt the normal flow of the story. For example, he tells the demons he has expelled and the people he has cured to be silent about the miraculous cures (1:34, 1:44, 3:12, 5:43, 7:36, 8:26). He even tells his disciples not to spread the news of his miraculous power (8:30, 9:9). The reason for these interruptions and this "secret" about his true nature and power as the Son of God is simple: Mark realized what people demanded and expected from Jesus. They wanted a powerful, earthly king. Mark knew that they had not understood the meaning of Jesus' life, death and resurrection. He wanted to set them on the right path. The result: Jesus often says, "Don't tell anyone about my power."

There can be no doubt that there was a good deal of fanatical enthusiasm among Jesus' followers after his resurrection. Many were convinced that heaven had come on earth, that Jesus' cross had been annulled, and that they were living in the kingdom of God already. God inspired Mark to see the effects and meaning of Jesus' death and resurrection differently. For Mark, Jesus' power and kingdom could only be *fully* established when he would come again in glory at the end of time (8:38). It is true that Jesus' kingdom had been begun. But until the Son of Man would come in glory, the Church's path would be difficult. After all, the Church's life on earth was (*and still is*) similar to the life of its master when he walked the earth: difficult, yet full of promise.

IN THESE FEW PARAGRAPHS I HAVE TRIED TO SUMMARIZE some of the more important background information that scholars give us about Mark, his times, his audience, and his purpose in writing the first gospel. Whenever we hear Mark's name, or begin to read from his gospel, we should pause for a second and place ourselves in that time of crisis and persecution, some 40 years after the death and resurrection of Jesus, when the early church needed an explanation of their suffering. We should remember that Mark challenged his people (and us) to believe that the way of the cross of Jesus was an essential part of the genuine good news ("gospel") and revelation of God.

Mark asked a question of the early church that is still a vital question asked of all Christians by God today: are we prepared, as Jesus of Nazareth was, to lay down our lives and power in order to serve God and others humbly, even unto death?

STEP TWO: A LOOK AT THE WHOLE GOSPEL OF MARK. HOW DOES MARK'S GOSPEL BEGIN AND END? WHERE DOES IT REACH ITS CLIMAX? HOW DOES HE PRESENT JESUS AND THE OTHER LEADING CHARACTERS? WHAT ARE THE BASIC RECURRING QUESTIONS THAT MARK DEALS WITH?

Before reading the gospel from beginning to end in one sitting, I ask you now to take a pencil and your Bible in hand. Please make notations in your Bible as I point out to you some of the literary artistry that scholars have discovered in Mark's gospel. Such activity on our part will be like a preview that will help you enjoy and understand the gospel as Mark intended you to.

THE BEGINNING

The first verse of the gospel is actually its title. It is "the gospel of Jesus Christ, *the Son of God*." In this first verse Mark brings his star on the stage and tells every reader who he is. You might underline that last phrase, however, because a quick glance through the entire script will reveal that *Mark is the only human being* ever to refer to Jesus as the Son of God, with one exception: the centurion at the foot of the cross (15:39). Every other human being, even Peter, is blind and unable to say or do what must be said and done! (You will note that the Father calls Jesus his Son; the devils frequently refer to him in this way too.)

In beginning as he does, Mark has given us a clue to the purpose and meaning of his whole gospel. For Mark realized that no one who lived with Jesus really understood him as he wished to be understood: i.e., no one could see him as the Son of God until they believed in him as the Suffering Messiah dying on the cross.

THE ENDING

Mark planned his ending as carefully as he planned his first verse. Now it is never fair to tell someone "how it ends." However, it is necessary and helpful to know that the curtain comes down on Mark's gospel after verse 8 of chapter 16. Notice please that there are many verses that follow verse 8. Then, please place a large period in your Bible after c.16v.8, after the women leave the tomb, afraid and trembling. For this is where Mark's gospel really ended. The vocabulary and style found in the verses that follow verse 8 argue strongly that they were written later by someone other than Mark and subsequently added to his gospel. This is important to know if the reader is to see that Mark's ending is as fascinating as his beginning. For as his gospel ends, Mark still leaves Christian of the 20th century in the same situation in which he left his audience in the 1st century. He doesn't "prove" that Jesus rose from the dead by giving us any accounts of post-resurrection appearances as the other evangelists do (e.g. the appearances of the risen Jesus to Mary Magdalen, to the disciples at Emmaus, etc.). Rather, he asks us: will you turn off your reading light "bewildered and trembling, and because of your great fear, say nothing to anyone" (16:8)? Or will you truly believe in the Son of God, which means not to give up hope in God's saving acts despite severe tensions, sufferings, failures, and death itself, but to hold fast to the belief that God will and can save even through death, as he saved his Son Jesus?

THE CLIMAX

Mark's gospel actually has two climaxes: the last scene of the women at the empty tomb (16:1-8) and the scene at Caesarea Philippi (8:27-38) where Peter says: "You are the Messiah!" (8:29). Peter gives the right answer to

Jesus' question, "Who am I?". However, almost immediately he tells Peter, "Get behind me, Satan!" For it is one thing to recognize Jesus as the Messiah, the one sent from God to bring men to God; but it is quite another thing to accept the challenge to follow that Messiah all the way to Jerusalem and the cross. "If *anyone* wishes to come after me, he must deny his very self, take up his cross, and follow in my steps" (8:34ff.). As the suffering Messiah goes, so must go the true Christian—all the way to the calvary of sacrificial union and communion with the Father and his fellow men. And where was Peter on calvary?

I ask you to mark off this climactic section of the gospel, for it is like the hinge that allows a door to be opened. Prior to this point, Jesus has not taught any explicit doctrine. Now he tells his disciples about his coming death (8:31ff.). He has taught in parables, but no one understood him (c.4). He has performed many powerful miracles (cc.1-8), but Jesus emerges as the most misunderstood person after such deeds. E.g., after curing the leper in Chapter 1, the cured man disobeyed Jesus' command that he *not* tell anyone about it. In fact, he told *everyone*! As a result of this it was no longer possible for Jesus to enter a town openly (1:45).

After the dramatic revelation at Caesarea Philippi in Chapter 8, Jesus teaches very clearly about how difficult it will be to follow him: he speaks forcefully about ambition and envy (9:33ff.), divorce (10:2-12), and the danger of riches (10:17ff.). Still, the disciples remain blind to Jesus' mission and his way. We can imagine the frustration of Jesus as James and John say: "See to it that we sit, one at your right hand and the other at your left, when you come into your glory" (10:37). They still don't understand as Jesus sadly replies: "Can you drink the cup I shall drink, or be baptized in the same bath of pain as I? The Son of Man has come, not to be served, but to serve—to give up his life in ransom for the many" (10:35-45). Remember who was with him as he drank the cup, at the foot of the cross. Not James, not John, not Peter. Only a few women and others looking on from a distance (15:37ff.). Jesus is left with a mission and destiny which he alone wants to accept. The others don't understand it! At his death, perhaps only he could accept and understand this. But what about now? Mark asks if his suffering Christians (in 70 A.D. and now) are as blind as Peter, James, and John. Are we?

THE HUMAN JESUS

Jesus is the Son of God. Mark assures us of this in his opening verse and in the many miracle stories. But Mark seems most at home when he paints the picture of the human Jesus.

Please briefly glance at (and perhaps mark off) the following sections of the gospel with me. In 5:30, Jesus was so human that he didn't know who had touched him when the lady with the hemorrhage had been cured. Jesus didn't know when the day of judgment would come (13:32). And Jesus wasn't only deficient in knowledge: he couldn't work miracles in Nazareth (6:5)! Jesus is also a very emotional person. More than once he was angry, grieved, or indignant (1:41; 3:5). He sighed deeply at the misunderstanding of the Pharisees (8:12) and disciples. He put up with the disciples who chided, scolded, and admonished him (10:13f). He slept as they almost drowned (4:38). Yet compassion brought on the miracle of the loaves and fishes (6:34). It was a tender love that reminded the parents of the twelve-year-old risen girl to get her some food (5:43). It was deep contact with his fellow man that urged him to eat with public sinners (2:13-17). Yes, Jesus was human enough to feel sleepy, hungry, upset, misunderstood, sorrowful, etc., just as we often feel. It is such a person that emerges as we glance at Jesus as Mark presents him: most human, yet obviously divine. This is the model and leader of the Church of 70 A.D. and of all ages.

THE BLIND DISCIPLES

According to Mark, it is clear that the disciples had failed to understand Jesus before his passion and death. Their lack of faith and vision was evident, above all, in their refusal to accept Jesus' teaching about his preordained suffering (8:31-33; 9:10; 9:32; 10:32). Consequently, they couldn't see his true nature in spite of his glorious acts. "On the contrary, their minds were completely closed to the meaning of the events" (6:52); events like Jesus' walk on the water and feeding of the five thousand (6:33-51). They had eyes but no sight, ears but no hearing. They saw and heard, but didn't understand (8:14-21)!

As we prepare to enter into dialogue with Jesus as Mark presents him, let us ask if our vision and understanding of the Christian life is that much different from Jesus' disciples (in 30 A.D.) or Mark's disciples (in 70 A.D.): do we too fail to see that he asks us to drink the same cup he did? Do we see that our role as Christians is like his, to serve and not to be served? Do we understand that if we really want to follow him, we too must die? Peter and the disciples refused to commit themselves to Jesus as he revealed himself to them. They had eyes but no sight. Are we blind disciples, 20th century vintage?

MARK'S PREOCCUPATION WITH THE EUCHARIST

I would like to help you be ready to appreciate one final important recurring theme that

Mark has artistically woven into his gospel: his preoccupation with the Eucharist under the figures of bread and the cup. Mark's gospel truly leads to the altar. For it has long been observed that he has connected the few verses that describe the Last Supper (14:17-31) to the rest of his gospel.

As you read chapters 6 through 8, count the times that Mark mentions bread or food (15 times). Bread only appears one more time in the remaining eight chapters (in 14:22, at the Last Supper, when he says: "Take this, this is my Body"). This intricate arrangement of all the miracles involving bread (in ch. 6-8), leading up to Jesus' call to communion with His Body on the night his passion began (in ch. 14), does not allow the Christian reader to understand either Jesus' miracles or the Eucharist without seeing them in the light of Jesus' true identity: the Suffering Servant who gives life through death, the one who feeds his people by offering them his own Body. (Paul Achtemeier has attempted to show that Mark has "reworked" two pre-existing series of miracle stories to lead his readers to a more appropriate and realistic understanding of the Eucharist, the cross, and the resurrection. Cf. "Toward the Isolation of Pre-Markan Miracle Catenae," *Journal of Biblical Literature*, vol. 89, pp. 265-291).

Likewise, Mark sums up the life of any true Christian when he equates Jesus' cup with the cross. The cup only appears in three instances in the whole gospel. You might underline them in your text: 10:38ff., 14:23, and 14:36. These three key passages show the Christian reader that each time he drinks of the cup of the Eucharist, he commits himself, as Jesus did, to suffering service of others unto death.

WE'VE TALKED ENOUGH *ABOUT* MARK AND HIS GOSPEL. Now is the time to read the whole gospel of Mark *in one sitting*. It should take about one hour. Please have the following questions at hand to help you BEFORE, DURING, and AFTER the reading.

ASSIGNMENT AND DISCUSSION QUESTIONS FOR CHAPTER 2.
(Jot your initial responses and reflections down; after the reading you can share these with others who will also be reading the gospel).

BEFORE THE READING
Reflect once more on who the inspired author was, who his audience was and what the overriding purpose of his creation was. (Step 1)

As you begin to read, can you identify with the members of Mark's community who first read this gospel in 65-70 A.D.? I.e., do you have any similar problems in understanding why you suffer, who Jesus really is for you, etc?

DURING THE READING

Does the person of Jesus emerge as a powerful but misunderstood person? Where?

How does Mark characterize the disciples, especially Peter? Where?

Where does Jesus' humanity stand out most for you in the gospel? Give chapter and verses.

Do you experience the progression of the drama and sense the double climax of chapter 8 and chapter 16?

AFTER THE READING

How do you relate to the Jesus that Mark presents in the gospel? Is there anything about Jesus in Mark's gospel that you never noticed or thought of before?

Are you more like the disciples or the centurion at the foot of the cross, as far as your faith goes?

According to Mark's gospel, what does it mean to be a follower of Jesus today? Choose one or two passages that best describe a follower of Jesus.

Which passage in the gospel best summarizes for you who Jesus is? Why?

3. THE LEPER AND THE MISUNDERSTOOD MESSIAH
Mark 1:40-45

AFTER YOU HAVE FIRST SPENT SOME BRIEF TIME with an attractive and stimulating person, you look forward to the next time you shall meet. Likewise, if you have invested your time and prayerful energy in Chapters 1 and 2, and if you have been stimulated and attracted by Mark and his "good news" about Jesus, you now want more. So let's spend some more time with Mark and Jesus as we examine the miracle story of the leper (1:40-45) in a careful, prayerful, and critical way (5 STEPS).

Please read the text:

40 A leper approached him with a request, kneeling down as he addressed him: "If you will to do so, you can cure me." 41 Moved with pity, Jesus stretched out his hand, touched him, and said: "I do will it. Be cured." 42 The leprosy left him then and there, and he was cured. 43 Jesus gave him a stern warning and sent him on his way. 44 "Not a word to anyone now," he said. Go off and present yourself to the priest and offer for your cure what Moses prescribed. That should be a proof for them." 45 The man went off and began to proclaim the whole matter freely,

making the story public. As a result of this, it was no longer possible for Jesus to enter a town openly. He stayed in desert places; yet people kept coming to him from all sides.

(From New American Bible translation)

STEP 1. BACKGROUND FACTS.

This text comes from the gospel of Mark, written about 70 A.D. Recall that Mark most likely never saw Jesus, and thus wasn't with him when this miracle took place. It was one of the many miracle stories that Mark gathered as he composed his gospel. And he didn't relate it to make sure that people would remember these amazing facts about Jesus. Rather, he was trying to deepen the faith of the early Christian Church: for if *Jesus* was crucified, after such powerful healings as this, why is Mark's community living in such confusion and fear in 70 A.D. as *they* suffer persecution and face death? Mark realized that his community of believers didn't understand WHO JESUS WAS (=SUFFERING MESSIAH) and WHAT JESUS' WAY WAS (=THE CROSS). He reminded these early Christians that faith in Jesus never meant that suffering and pain would be swept away. In fact, Mark wrote to explain that his Christians' suffering was an essential sign of the true follower of Jesus---

the one who came into glory *only after* the ignominious death on Calvary. The Christians' hope for resurrection glory and peace and healing could be realized only in following their Lord on his way. "From the cup I drink of you shall drink" (Mark 10:39).

When we remind ourselves of these background facts from the outset, we can reread our miracle story and understand why Jesus said: "Not a word to anyone now." Why? Because all the publicity about it would be aimed at making Jesus a "cure-all miracle-worker" who would alleviate all problems, for all people! Jesus knew better, says Mark. He had to die. . . but who would "come to him from all sides" as he hung on the cross? Who would believe in a Suffering Savior? Who would follow him on his way?

STEP 2. SEEING MARK 1:40-45 IN THE WHOLE

Figure 2, page opposite, is a diagram of the movement of Mark's whole gospel, as we considered it in Chapter 2, where we discussed Mark's two climaxes.

When we locate our section*(1:40-45) in this diagram of the whole gospel, we realize two important things:

First, this miracle story appears very early in the whole drama. It is, in fact, the third

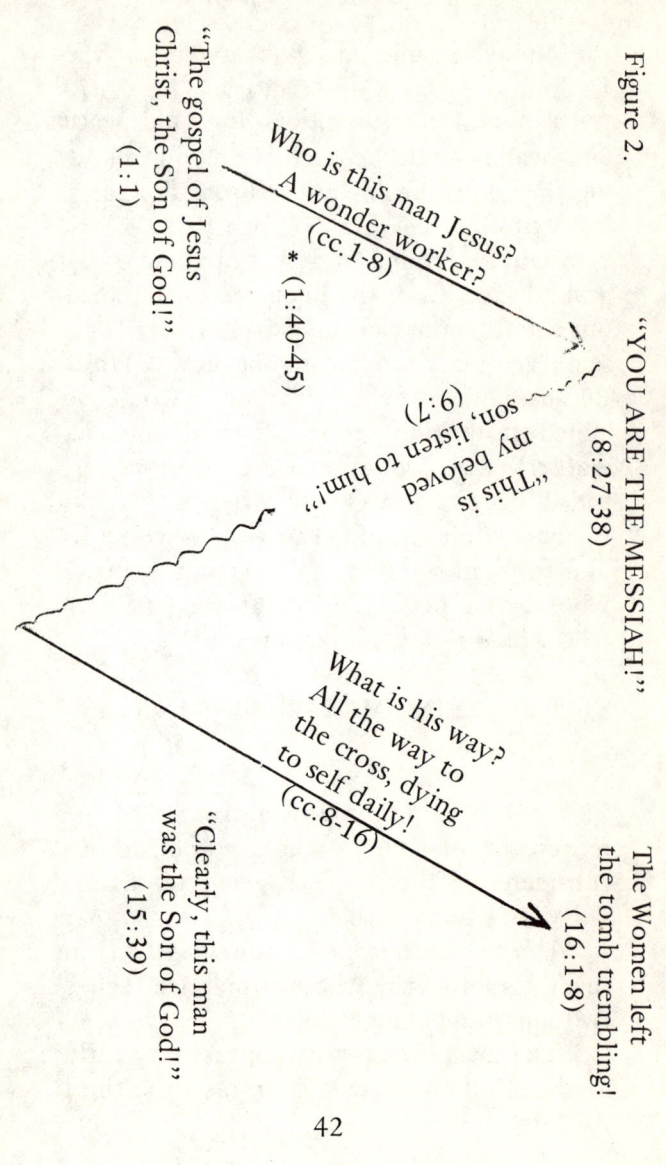

Figure 2.

miracle of Jesus to be related in detail. Thus, we see that Jesus is *misunderstood even as he begins* to reveal himself in his powerful healing and preaching (1:21-45). His early work among the crowds and Jews causes conflict (1:14-3:6). Consequently, as Mark seeks to reveal WHO JESUS IS (cc. 1-8:26), he is seen as powerful, but also as very misunderstood and hindered in his mission.

Secondly, by forcing ourselves to look at the whole gospel again, we recall its ending. Why pretend we don't see the implications of this early episode? Jesus will powerfully be raised from the dead—but will anyone understand his true identity and his way and its implications for all Christians? The leper *disobeyed* Jesus and *publicized* the miracle-worker's deed (1:45). The women will *disobey* the angel and *not publicize* the good news of his resurrection. . . for "they left the empty tomb bewildered and afraid, and said nothing to anyone" (16:8). Will Mark's audience disobey Jesus' call to true Christianity in 70 A.D.? In the 20th century?

STEP 3. COMPARING LOOK-ALIKES
    Mark 1:40-45, Matthew 8:1-4
    and Luke 5:12-16.

If you have your *New American Bible* open to Mark 1:40-45, you also can find where this story appears in the gospels of Matthew and

Luke quite easily. Notice the box at the bottom of the page in your Bible. There you find chapter and verse numbers. Look for the verse numbers 40-44 of chapter 1. After these numbers you will find the following: *Mt 8,2ff; Lk 5,12ff*. Now turn to those chapters in Matthew and Luke and you will see the *same* story as *they* present it.

For convenience sake I have presented here (in Figure 3) the three accounts as they appear in a *synopsis*. Please try to figure out for yourself what the *underscored* differences bring out about Mark's Jesus and Mark's intention in presenting the story in this way. After you've done this, you can check your ideas with mine (which follow).

Figure 3.

42. The Cleansing of the Leper

Matt. 8.1-4	Mark 1.40-45	Luke 5.12-16
1 *When he came down from the mountain, great crowds followed him*: 2 and behold /a leper came to him and knelt before him, saying, "*Lord*, if you will, you can make me clean" 3 And he stret-	40 And a leper came to him beseeching him, and kneeling said to him, "If you will, you can make me clean." 41 *Moved with pity*, he stretched out his hand and touched him, and said to him,	12 *While he was in one of the cities*, there came a man full of leprosy; and when he saw Jesus, he fell on his face and besought him, "*Lord*, if you will, you can make me clean" 13 And he stret-

ched out his hand and touched him, saying, "I will; be clean." And immediately his leprosy was cleansed.

4 And Jesus said to him, "See that you say nothing to any one; but go, show yourself to the priest and offer the gift that Moses commanded, for a proof to the people."

"I will; be clean." 42 And immediately the leprosy left him, and he was made clean. 43 *And he sternly charged him, and sent him away at once*, 44 and said to him, "See that you say nothing to any one; but go, show yourself to the priest and offer for your cleansing what Moses commanded, for a proof to the people." 45 *But he went out and began to talk freely about it, and to spread the news, so that Jesus could no longer openly enter a town, but was out in the country and people came to him from every quarter.*

ched out his hand and touched him, saying, "I will; be clean." And immediately the leprosy left him.

14 And he charged him to tell no one; but "go and show yourself to the priest, and make an offering for your cleansing, as Moses commanded, for a proof to the people." 15 But so much the more the report went abroad concerning him; and great multitudes gathered to hear and to be healed of their infirmities. 16 But he withdrew to the wilderness *and prayed.*

COMPARING THE THREE ACCOUNTS we see some differences right away. They seem small and insignificant, but are they? For example, in the first verse of each account we see two differences:

Matthew 8:1	Mark 1:40	Luke 5:12
1) coming from mount	----------------	in a city
2) Jesus is LORD	Jesus is ?	Jesus is LORD

Moreover, in the dialogue with the leper, Matthew and Luke fail to mention two characteristics of Mark's human Jesus: only Mark's Jesus is "moved with pity," and he alone "sternly charges the leper to go away at once" (vv.41 and 43). Finally, after the miracle both Matthew and Luke omit the disobedience of the leper and the consequent problematic popularity brought to Jesus. (Luke seems to see the popularity of Jesus as a *good* result of the miracle!)

Thus we see that the three evangelists seem to be emphasizing different things for their audiences. Matthew's Lord finishes the sermon on the mount (Mt. Chapters 5-7) and shows that Jesus' actions speak as loudly as his words by this miracle. Luke's Lord cures everyone and withdraws to pray (which is one of Luke's favorite activities of the Lord). Mark's Jesus (not called Lord) is very human, emotional, misunderstood, and his power creates problems for him (they want to make him king?).

Matthew and Luke smooth out the rough edges of the man Jesus as portrayed by Mark. They thought that Mark's account of the miracle showed Jesus to be too emotional. And the miracle caused too many problems for Jesus! However, that was precisely Mark's point: Jesus was both God *and man*. He had problems and emotions like us. And his mission was misunderstood from the beginning!

STEP 4. WHAT WAS GOD SAYING TO HIS PEOPLE THROUGH MARK 1:40-45, IN 70 A.D.

BECAUSE OF OUR PROFESSIONAL AND PERSONAL INVOLVEMENT with his Word we are now better prepared to hear what God intended to say to his people in 70 A.D. through St. Mark. We can hear God more clearly because we have tried to hear him speak in his own way, without immediately rushing to appropriate his message to our own place, time, language and world. He says:

MY BELOVED CHILDREN, CHRISTIANS OF 70 A.D.: YOU ARE HURTING AND REJECTED TODAY MUCH LIKE THE LEPER WAS SOME 40 YEARS AGO. YOU MAY NOT SEE JESUS' MYSTERIOUS HEALING ACTION AT WORK IN YOUR LIVES AT THIS MOMENT OF PERSEC-

UTION. BUT DON'T LOSE TRUST IN FOR HE IS MY SON AND YOUR POWERFUL, COMPASSIONATE LORD. HIS FIRST DISCIPLES THOUGHT THEY WERE FOLLOWING A WONDER-WORKER WHO WOULD BE KING. YOU KNOW THAT VERY FEW OF THEM FOLLOWED HIM TO THE LOWLINESS AND PAIN OF THE CROSS. ARE YOU WILLING TO FOLLOW HIM IN HIS SUFFERING, OR ONLY IN HIS GLORIOUS DEEDS?

Mark's account of the leper and Jesus is not meant to present an historical fact to be admired. He doesn't present the story to prove that Jesus was God . . . he and his readers already believed that. Rather, Mark presents the account to challenge his Christians to understand who Jesus really was (the suffering and misunderstood Messiah) and to trust in him. Do they? Will they?

STEP 5. WHAT DOES GOD SAY TO US TODAY THROUGH MARK 1:40-45?

We have invested much time and energy on these six verses. Where has it led? It has led us through critical questioning to understand precisely how Mark is challenging us to respond to God's Word today; we no longer need to wonder why Jesus told the cured leper *not* to tell people about the miracle. We know he is a healing, saving Lord. But we *also* realize that he works in our lives in *the way he wishes*. What is our sickness? Is it physical, like the leper's? Is it the feeling of being isolated and lonely, like the leper (who was an outcast of society)? Is it the feeling of being misunderstood, like Jesus himself felt?

In our confusion (the turbulent 70's, after the Vatican Council) do we trust in the man God who died for us, who suffered like we suffer, who calls us to be in union with him?

What does God say to us today through Mark 1:40-45? It is the same thing he said to his own people in 70 A.D.:

MY BELOVED CHILDREN, CHRISTIANS OF THE 20TH CENTURY: TRUST IN MY SAVING POWER. I UNDERSTAND YOU. I AM MOVED WITH PITY AND COMPASSION EVEN TODAY, AS I SEE YOU SUFFER. BE ONE WITH ME, AND EXPERIENCE THE POWER OF THE RESURRECTION IN THE WEAKNESS AND PAIN OF THE CROSS *YOU* BEAR. ON YOUR KNEES, SEE THE BROKEN BODY OF MY SON ON HIS CROSS. THEN REJOICE IN THE SALVATION AND CONSOLATION WHICH I OFFER YOU NOW, SO THAT YOU CAN LIVE YOUR LIVES AS MY SON LIVED HIS . . . HEALING OTHERS AND LEADING THEM TO ME.

ASSIGNMENT AND DISCUSSION QUESTIONS FOR CHAPTER 3.

1. Does the short miracle story of the leper mean more to you now than it did before you went through the 5 critical steps? What step brought out the most for you? Explain and share with other members of the study group.
2. Read Mark 8:27-34. After you read this passage from Mark's gospel, find the corresponding passages in Matthew and Luke. What are the major differences that you discover (Step 3)? (Be precise as you study the three similar passages for we shall take up Mark 8 next).

4. WHO DO YOU SAY THAT I AM?
Mark 8:27-38

Text, from *New American Bible*

27 Then Jesus and his disciples set out for the villages around Caesarea Philippi. On the way he asked his disciples this question: "Who do people say that I am?" 28 They replied, "Some, John the Baptizer, others Elijah, still others, one of the prophets." 29 "And you," he went on to ask, "Who do you say that I am?" Peter answered him, "You are the Messiah!" 30 Then he gave them strict orders not to tell anyone about him.

31 He began to teach them that the Son of Man had to suffer much, be rejected by the elders, the chief priests, and the scribes, be put to death, and rise three days later. 32 He said these things quite openly. Peter then took him aside and began to remonstrate with him. 33 At this he turned around and, eyeing the disciples, reprimanded Peter: "Get out of my sight, you satan! You are not judging by God's standards but by man's!"

34 He summoned the crowd with his disciples and said to them: "If a man wishes to come after me, he must deny his very self, take up his cross, and follow in my steps. 35 Whoever would preserve his life will lose it,

but whoever loses his life for my sake and the gospel's will preserve it. 36 What profit does a man show who gains the whole world and destroys himself in the process? 37 What can a man offer in exchange for his life? 38 If anyone in this faithless and corrupt age is ashamed of me and my doctrine, the Son of Man will be ashamed of him when he comes with the holy angels in his Father's glory."

STEP 1. BACKGROUND INFORMATION

In our world today millions of people are suffering and dying from hunger, hatred and war. Closer to home and our daily lives, each of us knows unhappy people who are slowly suffocating to death from loneliness, mental confusion, and from the misunderstanding of a spouse, a child, a parent, or friends. Such situations, often labeled "impossible," are not unique to our times. Nor are those people unique to our times who seriously reflect on the meaning of such situations and try to understand them and lovingly live them in the light of Jesus' message and deeds. Mark was one of these interpreters of life. You and I are trying to be like him. All of us are called Christians precisely because of this reflection on Christ and our consequent actions that flow from it.

In chapter 8, verses 27-38, Mark, the Christian pastor of the first century, reflects on the blindness of those closest to Jesus, Peter and the disciples. They regarded Jesus as a prophet or a Messiah. In Jesus' time (about 30 A.D.), the believers watched him as if he were a spectacular actor on the stage, curing all the sick and doing all things well (=the Messiah-Savior-Hero). Mark, who knows that Jesus *had to die* before the drama could be completed, reflects on the meaning of Jesus' life and question: "Who do *you* say that I am?" (Mark 8:29). He does this for himself and for his own times (70 A.D.). He sees that the spotlight has been turned off the stage and out into the gazing audience: "He summoned *the crowd* (Mark's audience and us) and the disciples and said *to them* (to us): if a man (not just Peter or the first disciples) wishes to come after me, he must deny his very self, take up his cross and follow in my steps. *Whoever* (not just some saint) would preserve his life will lose it, but *whoever* (in any age) loses his life for my sake and the gospel's will preserve it."

If we read Mark 8 critically, we realize that God has turned the spotlight on us, Christians of the 20th century. Are the lights too bright for us? Do we want to avoid their glare? Or will we see who Jesus is, and will we understand, as Peter didn't, the call to follow Jesus in his steps?

STEP 2. SEEING THE WHOLE GOSPEL

I hope that my artwork on the following page will depict for you the whole gospel of Mark "in a glance," highlighting the important transition that takes place in chapter 8. Please follow the arrows from beginning to end. Notice that Mark has placed most of the miracle stories about Jesus in the first half of his gospel (18 of them, signified in Figure 4. by X.). Then, after our scene in chapter 8, Mark's Jesus turns to all Christians and begins to preach clearly about what the Christian life really means (each of these teachings about the cross and the Christian life is signified in Figure 4. by a †). Please notice that there are only three miracle stories reported in the last eight chapters of his gospel (the cure of the possessed boy in c.9; the blind man in c.10; the Resurrection itself in c.16). Please study the whole gospel a la Leonardo Van Linden.

If we follow the plan of Mark from the beginning to the end of his gospel, a simple message emerges: there is no glory without the cross, for any Christian, including Jesus. That is, as Christ goes, so must go the *Christ*ian. Look at his miracles and listen to his words. Then, follow him with loving trust.

Here he comes!!
Who is this Jesus?
Peter says. "You are the Messiah!" (8:27-38)
John the Baptist prepares the way of the Lord!
"We know who he is: he is the powerful miracle worker – look at all his miracles!" (cc.1-8)
Jesus replies: "The Son of Man must suffer and die."
START (c.1)
"Jesus, you're crazy!" (Peter)
'HIS IS MY BELOVED SON: LISTEN TO HIM."
Hey! Guess what you have to do if you want to follow me!
END
Listen closely!! (cc.8-16)

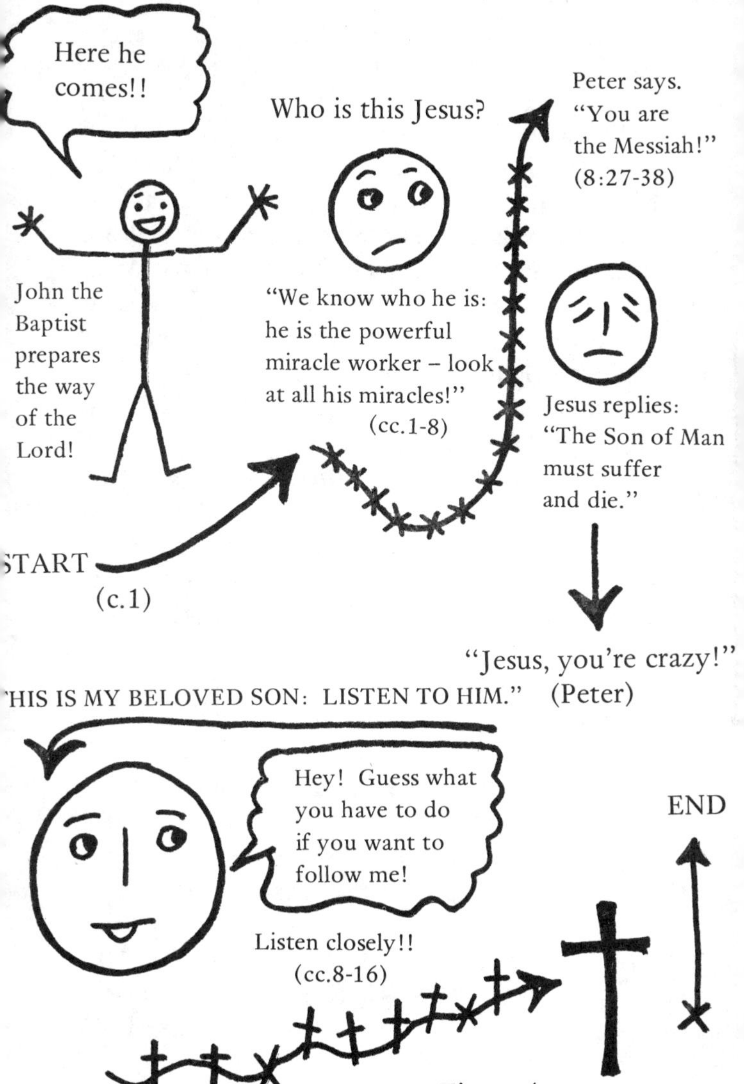

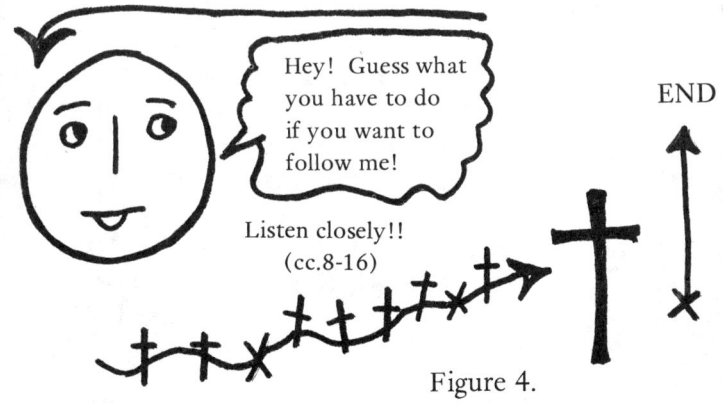

Figure 4.

STEP 3. COMPARING "LOOK-ALIKES"

Please place a marker in your Bible at Mark 8:27-38. Then, place markers at Matthew 16:13-28 and Luke 9:18-27. As you read each of these three accounts of the same event, please notice: 1. what Matthew has added to Mark; 2. what Luke has omitted from Mark; 3. that all three of the inspired authors *next* present the transfiguration, but that it is Mark alone who places the blind man's cure (8:22-26) just *before* our section.

As you flip back and forth in this synoptic comparison, isn't it rather clear that Matthew presents Peter, the Rock, in a more favorable light than Mark does? Doesn't Luke do something similar as he omits altogether the argument between Jesus and Peter? Isn't it curious that Mark alone balances off the glory of the Transfiguration (after our scene) with the gradual healing of a blind man (before our scene?) Is Mark trying to say something about Peter, even in the blind man story? What is God trying to say to us, through Mark, as the drama unravels unto death on the cross?

STEP 4. WHAT *WAS* GOD SAYING TO HIS FIRST CHRISTIAN READERS THROUGH MARK 8?

MY BELOVED CHILDREN,
YOU ARE AMONG THE FIRST WHO BELIEVE IN MY SON, WHO DIED FOR YOU OUT OF LOVE SOME FORTY YEARS AGO. YOU KNOW OF HIS POWER AND HIS RESURRECTION. YOU WISH TO FOLLOW HIM. ARE YOU READY TO CARRY YOUR CROSS AND DENY YOURSELVES LIKE HE DID? DO YOU SEE THAT YOUR FAITH, HOPE AND LOVE, LIKE HIS, ARE PROVEN IN FOLLOWING HIS WAY OF LOVING, EVEN WHEN IT LEADS TO DEATH? THE CHRISTIAN LIFE IS FULL OF HOPE, BUT NOT IF YOU REMAIN A SPECTATOR. THE SPOTLIGHT IS ON YOU NOW. "IF ANYONE WISHES TO FOLLOW JESUS . . . . . "

Mark could hardly have chosen a more difficult way to teach life: "to live is to die; in order to save your personhood, nail it to a cross; refuse, be refused." Yet Mark had proof that Jesus was right! Give up all in crucifixion for Christ and others---then you live!

STEP 5. WHAT *IS* GOD TELLING US TODAY, THROUGH MARK 8?

It takes courage to move away from a safe place into the unknown. It is scary to surrender ourselves to a person, even Jesus himself, when we know the surrender in love leads to the cross. Yet Jesus' was was the way of suffering as well as the way of love.

> MY CHILDREN OF THE 20TH CENTURY, IT OFTEN SEEMS PRETTY DARK AND CONFUSING AS YOU TRY TO BE MY SON'S FOLLOWERS. TO THE DEGREE THAT YOU FOLLOW HIM, YOU WILL LOVE MORE AND SUFFER MORE, YOU WILL SEE MORE LIGHT AND MORE DARKNESS, MORE OF HIM AND MORE OF HUMANITY. WHEN YOU HAVE JOINED HIM IN HIS ANGUISHING LOVE-LIFE FOR OTHERS, YOU WILL ALSO EXPERIENCE THE BEAUTY OF HIS TRANSFIGURATION AND THE POWER OF HIS RESURRECTION. THIS IS A GRADUAL PROCESS: BUT IF YOU ASK JESUS SINCERELY, HE WILL RESTORE YOUR SIGHT AND YOU WILL SEE THINGS CLEARLY. LISTEN TO HIM, FOR YOU KNOW WHO HE IS!

ASSIGNMENT AND DISCUSSION
QUESTIONS FOR CHAPTER 4.

Please extend your prayerful reflection about this key chapter in Mark's gospel over several days, pondering the following questions on successive days. Then, when you gather together in your discussion group, you will have much to share from your extended dialogue with God's Word.

FIRST DAY

Read Mark 8:22-9:8, and *record your reactions*, as if:
  a) you were Peter;
  b) you were one of the other disciples;
  c) you were Jesus himself.

How do you feel (as Peter, a disciple, or Jesus) out there "on the stage"?

SECOND DAY

Glance at the great number of miracles in chapters 1-8, and then *record* the *miracles* found *after chapter 8* (by chapter and verse numbers). Although they are few in number, these miracles in the later chapters certainly have a special emphasis. What is it?

Glance at the many clear teachings of Jesus (especially in chapters 9 and 10), and then *record* the few times that Jesus *teaches* anything *in chapters 1-8* (by chapter and verse numbers). Although Jesus does teach a few times in these earlier chapters, how often does anyone understand what he is saying?

Reflect on how you habitually relate to Jesus. Do you see him as a powerful wonder-worker, only? Or are you one that truly listens to what he has to say (about status, ambition, money, marriage, etc)? Do you understand him and his power in the light of his very demanding teaching and death? Can you pray with such a person? Do you? Will you?

THIRD DAY

Read Mark 8:27-38, and after praying to the forceful but misunderstood Jesus who emerges, *write him a letter* about the way you feel toward him.

FOURTH DAY

In your own words, *record* what God is urging you *to realize* and *to do* through this passage, and through chapters 9 and 10 which are so closely related to it. In your concerete daily experience of life, who do you say that he is?

(In the LEADERS' GUIDE you will find recorded some of the realizations and resolutions that others have arrived at after their prayerful study of this section of Mark's gospel.)

5. FOLLOWING JESUS ALL THE WAY---TODAY: MARK 10.

STEP 1. BACKGROUND INFORMATION.

An enthusiastic group of Catholic adults gathers around the parish priest, planning a series of discussions on issues which are important today. These concerned Christians want to discuss marriage and the family, poverty and justice. They want to find out how they should respond to situations that cause so much agony. They want to share their ideas and to act as Jesus would, if he were here today. The pastor suggests they look to the Scriptures for some guidance. They discover there, especially in chapter 10 of Mark's gospel, that a similar meeting took place some nineteen hundred years ago, with Mark as the pastor. These modern-day Christians immediately sense a union with the earliest Christians as they examine the conclusions that Mark's community arrived at when they tried to follow Jesus in the problematic areas of: marriage and divorce, riches, and status in the comminity.

It is a commonly held opinion among Scripture scholars today that chapter 10 of Mark's gospel tells us more about the existential situation of the early Christian community than most other sources do. In this chapter we hear Jesus dialoguing with his disciples about divorce (vv.2-12), about possessions (vv.17-31), and about status in the community, i.e.,"who's first?" (vv.35-45). Each of these dialogues between Jesus and his disciples makes drastic demands of the first followers (30 A.D.). But the scholars see more. They see that Mark has updated Jesus' teachings to meet the concrete needs of his own community, some forty years after Jesus' life (70 A.D.). It is the scholars' conclusion that Mark has taken the very demanding "Jesus traditions" about divorce, possessions and precedence; and after seeing how his own community was being divided and hurt over similar issues, he adapted this collection of rules and sayings to the problem of suffering in his own Christian community. In so doing he was concretely challenging his contemporary Christians to follow Jesus on his suffering and loving way, in their own daily experience of life. Consequently, chapter 10 specifies for Mark's Christians what it means to "Take up their crosses, and follow in his steps" (vv.8:34).

Consequently, as we read and study chapter 10 prayerfully, we are in touch with believers on all four levels of the Critical Stage of studying God's Word (cf. Figure 1, on page 20). We are not only in union with modern-day concerned Catholics gathered around their parish priest. We are also in contact with Mark, with the early Christian community, and with Jesus himself.

STEP 2. SEEING CHAPTER 10 IN THE LIGHT OF THE WHOLE.

Several years ago I went to see the Swedish film, *Elvira Madigan*. As the movie began, I was surprised to hear a voice telling the audience that the movie was a true story of a 19th century couple, a married man, Count Sparre and Elvira Madigan, a lovely young tight-rope walker, who were one day found together shot in the woods. I felt like leaving. Why had the director "given the ending of the film away" before it had begun?

Moments later a young couple came in and sat in front of me. They got settled as the story began to unfold. Since they had missed the vital piece of information given at the beginning, they consequently viewed the entire film from a totally different perspective than the rest of us. Since they did *not* know this movie was a classic tragedy of love, they undoubtedly were wondering how it would all come out. The rest of us were able to appreciate the subtle, poetic beauty of the film. We experienced no sense of apprehension or doubt about the outcome of the events that unraveled before our eyes. Rather we were led to say to ourselves: "Poor Elvira and Count Sparre, if they had only been more careful there . . . ah, there's where the lovers made their mistake . . . etc."

The director wanted such active participation and such a response from his viewers. Without this sort of viewer involvement, the film was less inspiring, a rather idyllic love story. With it, everyone was thoroughly involved with the star-crossed lovers from the first minute. . .except the young couple who arrived slightly late. (Cf. DeRosa, *Jesus Who Became the Christ*, who discusses this further.)

Now, *we* know the ending of Mark's gospel already, because we have prayerfully read and studied the whole gospel. We know that Jesus had to die in the end, prior to rising from the dead. We also know that no one really expected his death or understood his teachings before Calvary. So, as we see the drama unfold (in ch. 10), we can appreciate what Jesus said and what he asked of his followers, better than his followers themselves did! After all, we know the ending. They didn't.

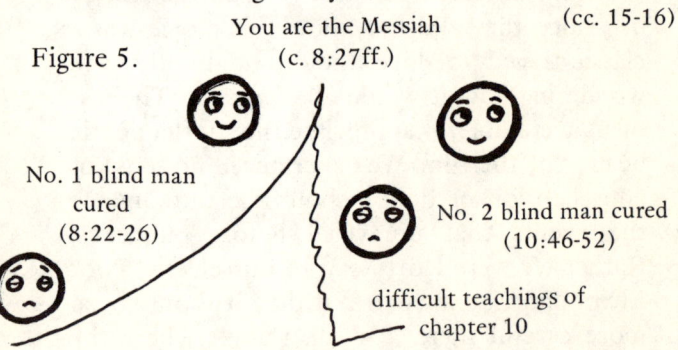

Figure 5.

You are the Messiah (c. 8:27ff.)

(cc. 15-16)

No. 1 blind man cured (8:22-26)

No. 2 blind man cured (10:46-52)

difficult teachings of chapter 10

Notice please that there are two cures of the blind in Mark's gospel (8:22-26; 10:46-52).

Figure 5 reminds us that the first cure immediately precedes the confession of Peter in chapter 8. Jesus had cured a man of his physical blindness, and yet Peter *couldn't see* (and wouldn't admit) that Jesus would have to suffer and die (8:22-8:38). The other blind man story precedes Jesus' entrance into Jerusalem where he is to die (10:46-11:11). This blind man, named Bartimaeus, is cured just after the most demanding part of Jesus' message for his followers: about marriage and divorce, about possessions and poverty, about ambition and true service (10:1-45).

Will Mark's readers be cured of their blindness? Will they choose to follow Jesus' demanding teachings (10:1-45)? Will they follow him on his way, as did Bartimaeus (10:52)? Or will they stand by as uninvolved observers, wondering aimlessly "how is this all going to end"? Or might they even say: "I hope this story ends pretty soon; I'm getting bored."

STEP 3. COMPARING "LOOK-ALIKES":
Mark 10, Matthew 19 and 20, Luke 18.

(For an excellent, detailed comparison of the synoptic gospels on these chapters, see Vawter, *The Four Gospels: An Introduction*, vol. II, pp. 83-126).

For our purposes here, I shall limit my observations to a brief comparison of Mark with

Matthew on two sections of chapter 10: the question of *status within the community* in Mk 10:35-45 / Mt 20:20-28, and *the curing of the blind man* in Mk 10:46-52 / Mt 20:29-34. (In the assignment that follows this chapter, I shall ask *you* to compare Mark and Matthew on the questions of divorce and riches.)

MARK 10:35-45 COMPARED WITH MATTHEW 20:20-28 – THE AMBITIOUS DISCIPLES,

Please read the two accounts in your Bible. You will see that they are the same except for one detail: Mark says that *James and John asked* for the best and second best places in the kingdom of God after Jesus himself (Mk 10:35). Matthew ascribes this ambition less directly to the apostles and rather to *their mother* (Mt 20:20). The proverbial aspirations which mothers entertain for their sons lends a familiar touch of human interest to Matthew's account of the story. Matthew's rendition is also consistent with his inclination to minimize the blindness and misunderstanding of the apostles, and to present them in a better light. He blames "momma" for putting such ideas into their heads.

No matter who asked Jesus "who would be first," the message of the encounter is clear in both Mark and Matthew: true followers of

Jesus are not to be concerned about being in positions of authority over others. It is true that every organization, even the Church, must have its leaders. But the Church's leaders, indeed *all* Christians, are called to be loving servants of others, as was Jesus, the servant of all (Mk 10:44-45 and Mt 20:26-28).

MARK 10:46-52 COMPARED WITH MATTHEW 20:29-34: THE BLIND MAN (MEN) CURED.

After reading the two accounts of this miracle, you will find one major discrepancy: the number of the blind men who figure in the story. For Mark (and also Luke, in Lk 18:35-43) there is only one blind man, called Bartimaeus. Matthew has two blind men.

A quick glance through the whole gospel of Matthew will show that he has omitted the other blind man story of Mark 8:22-26. Perhaps Matthew has joined the two accounts together here in order to have two blind men (instead of just one) shout out "Jesus is the Son of David" (20:30), as Jesus prepares for his triumphal entry into Jerusalem. This lends prominence to this momentous event.

Once again, in spite of the differing details, Mark and Matthew are *both concerned with one thing*: the person who believes that Jesus is the Son of David (and Son of God) will be cured of blindness and will respond by following Jesus to Jerusalem (=his loving death on the cross as servant of all).

STEP 4. WHAT *WAS* GOD SAYING TO THE EARLY CHRISTIANS IN 70 A.D. THROUGH MARK 10:35-52?

MY BELOVED CHILDREN,
IF YOU WISH TO BE CHRISTIAN LEADERS WORTHY OF THE NAME, YOU WILL SHARE IN THE SUFFERING AND DEATH (CUP) OF JESUS MY SON. BUT THERE IS MORE: YOU ARE ALSO TO LIVE LIKE HIM, *FOR CHRISTIAN LIFE MEANS SERVICE.* PUT ALL OF THIS TOGETHER, AS DID MY SON, THEN YOU WILL SEE THAT REAL LEADERSHIP AND GREATNESS LIES IN PATIENT SUFFERING IN THE SERVICE OF OTHERS. ARE YOU STILL BLIND, OR CAN YOU NOW SEE THAT? WILL YOU FOLLOW MY LOVING SON, WHO GAVE HIS LIFE IN RANSOM FOR MANY? ARE YOU REALLY CHRISTIANS?

STEP 5. WHAT IS GOD ASKING OF US TODAY?

MY BELOVED SONS AND DAUGHTERS,
BY BAPTISM IN WATER, ALL OF YOU HAVE BECOME MEMBERS OF MY SON'S

CHURCH, THE BODY OF CHRIST. BUT THIS MEMBERSHIP IS NOT LIKE A FREE PASS INTO GLORY. YOU ARE CALLED TO BE MEMBERS OF A SERVANT CHURCH. YOU ARE CALLED TO GIVE OF YOURSELF FOR OTHERS. YOU ARE TO CARE FOR THE NEEDS OF OTHERS. YOU ARE TO LOVE THEM, EVEN IF IT HURTS.

ARE YOU BLINDED BY VISIONS OF GLORY, RICHES, AND EASY CHRISTIANITY? OR DO YOU SEE YOUR LORD AS SERVANT? AND DO YOU HELP MAKE THE CHURCH A LOVING SERVANT BY TAKING THE INITIATIVE TO REACH OUT TO THOSE IN NEED ALL AROUND YOU?

ASSIGNMENT AND DISCUSSION
   QUESTIONS FOR CHAPTER 5.

(There are five questions below. Please consider one a day.)

FIRST DAY
   After the 5-step study of the ambitious disciples and the blind man (Mark 10:35-52) what do you choose to do this week/month to be a true follower of Jesus. That is, *how* will *you* serve your needy brothers and sis-

ters in your parish? *Who are* the needy ones in your parish?

SECOND DAY

How is your parish proving itself to be a living witness of the Servant Christ and the Servant Church? Is there any organization that truly empties itself for others? How can you assist your parish priests in making the local Church a more living and loving Servant of God's people?

THIRD DAY

Compare Mark 10:2-10 and Matthew 19:3-9 on the question of divorce.
  a) What are the major differences?
  b) How does Matthew seem to "soften" Mark's account?
  c) What is the major message common to both accounts?
  d) What does God say to you through Mark?

FOURTH DAY

Compare Mark 10:17-31 with Matthew 19:16-30 on the question of riches.
  a) What are the major differences?
  b) How does Matthew seem to "soften" Mark's message?
  c) What is the major message common to both?

d) What does God say to you through Mark?

FIFTH DAY

We have seen how a later inspired author (Matthew, writing in 80 A.D.) has adapted and developed the gospel teachings on divorce and riches as he found them in the gospel of an earlier inspired author (Mark, 70 A.D.). With that in mind, do you have a better idea of how the Church adapts and develops the gospel teachings today?

SIXTH DAY

Every time you go to Mass, you hear Christ the high priest say: "Take this, all of you and eat it; this is my Body." "Take this, all of you and drink from it; this is the cup of my Blood ... " At communion time you receive the Body and Blood of Christ under the form of bread. Sometimes (e.g., at weddings) some of you drink from the cup also. Please reflect on the deep meaning of Christ's invitation to all of us: that we all commit ourselves to drinking from the same cup of suffering as he did, in loving service of others; that we all follow him all the way —today.

(As you reflect on this profound reality, please also read Mark 10:38ff., 14:23ff., and 14:36ff. These are the *only* three places in Mark's gospel that the cup is mentioned.)

CONCLUSION

In the *First Letter to the Thessalonians*, which is considered to be one of the earliest Christian documents we have, St. Paul tells his brother and sister Christians: "We thank God constantly that in receiving his message from us you took it, not as the word of men, but as it truly is, the word of God at work within you" (I Thess. 2:13). In our own day, some 2,000 years later, Pope Paul VI and the Bishops of Vatican II have spoken similarly in the *Dogmatic Constitution on Divine Revelation*:

> The Church has always regarded, and continues to regard the Scriptures, taken together with sacred Tradition, as the supreme rule of her faith . . . In the sacred books the Father who is in heaven comes lovingly to meet his children, and talks with them. And such is the force and power of the Word of God that it can serve the Church as her support and vigor, and the Children of the Church as strength for their faith, food for the soul, and a pure and lasting fount of spiritual life (Par. 21 of Divine Revelation, *Vatican Council II*, p.762).

The Council Fathers not only encouraged that "access to sacred Scripture be open wide to the Christian faithful"; they also make it very clear that "the interpreter of Scripture, if he is to ascertain what God has wished to communicate to us, should carefully search out the meaning which the sacred writers really had in mind, that meaning which God had thought well to manifest through the medium of their words" (Par. 12, Divine Revelation, *Vatican Council II*, p.757).

In this booklet I have tried to help you, who are hungry for the nourishing Word of God, to understand the basic principles of Scripture study, especially as they pertain to the work of St. Mark, the sacred author of the first gospel. If you have found my words helpful, and if you have been motivated to enter into an enriching dialogue *with God himself* in the sixteen inspired chapters of Mark's gospel, then I too thank God that you have received his message as it truly is, the Word of God at work within you.

FOR FURTHER STUDY

Concerning Mark's Gospel:

Nineham, D.E. *Saint Mark*, The Pelican Gospel Commentaries (Penguin Books: 1963), 477pp., available in paperback through most bookstores.

Schenke, Ludger. *Glory and the Way of the Cross: The Gospel of Mark*. Herald Biblical Booklets (Franciscan Herald Press: 1972),

72 pp., 95c, available from Franciscan Herald Press, 1434 W. 51st St., Chicago, Illinois 60609.

Both of these excellent paperbacks are most readable and available. They fill in much of the background to Mark's gospel. Nineham's classic commentary gives a detailed and simple summary of scholars' opinions about every verse of the gospel.

Concerning Mark, Matthew, Luke (and John)

Ciuba, Edward. *Who Do You Say That I Am?* (Alba House: 1974), paper.

Vawter, Bruce. *The Four Gospels: An Introduction*, 2 vols. (Image, 1967). Available in paperback.

These paperbacks present rich insights about each of the gospels. Fr. Ciuba's work is a fine adult study guide on the first three gospels, while Fr. Vawter presents all four gospels side by side, bringing out their special emphasis through a thorough synoptic comparison (our STEP 3). Both are worth purchasing.

The Jerome Biblical Commentary (Prentice Hall: 1968), 1524 pp.

This is the most complete Catholic commentary on sacred scripture available today.

It deals with every aspect of biblical studies, from more general background information to a detailed analysis of every verse in the Bible. Although it is expensive (about $36), it is indispensable. If you cannot afford it personally, you should urge those responsible to purchase it for your parish library.

Introductory Material

Bornkamm, Gunter. *The New Testament: A Guide to Its Writings* (Fortress Press: 1973), 161 pp., paper.

Schokel, Alonso. *Understanding Biblical Research* (Herder and Herder: 1968), 130 pp., paper.

Bornkamm's introduction to the New Testament gives a capsule summary of all recent scholarly study, treating every author of the New Testament in simple detail. Father Schokel presents the history of the biblical movement in such a way that it can be clearly and sympathetically understood by all.

Rome and the Study of Scripture (Abbey Press: 1964), 176 pp., paper.

Vatican Council II: The Conciliar and Post Conciliar Documents A. Flannery, O.P., General Editor (Franciscan Herald Press, Chicago: 1975), 1062 pp., paper.

Both of these books are rich sources for the teachings of the Church on matters of scripture and Christian life.

Text

The New American Bible (various publishers: 1970).
After 25 years of work by American Catholic scripture scholars, this translation is the best available today. Moreover, its footnotes and brief introductions to each book of the Bible alone are worth the price.

LEADER'S GUIDE

Suggested answers and aides for discussion questions:

Concerning Chapter 1 (found on p.23)

1. The melody and words of a song like "Follow Me" are beautiful and meaningful in themselves. However, knowing something about the performer, Mary Travers (cf.p.12) helps one to hear another level of meaning in the words: that very real personal cry of one who needs a friend at this time in her real life.

   Another example of the importance of knowing the identity of an author: "John said that we could all count on him." What a difference when we find out that John is: President John Kennedy, or John Mitchell, or Pope John XXIII, or Johnny Bench (hitting catcher of the Cincinnati Reds)!

2. When presented with a family crisis or a student-teacher conflict, a good counsellor wishes to hear "both sides of the story"; i.e., the whole story. Then he/she can truly understand why a certain situation is like it is, and can be of assistance to those in trouble (cf. p.14).

3. (Cf. pp. 15-17) The gospels of Matthew, Mark, and Luke contain many similar stor-

ies and words of Jesus. One notes that almost 600 verses of Mark's gospel (it contains only 661 verses) reappear in Matthew's gospel). (330 of Mark's verses are found also in Luke's gospel). This seems to point to the fact that Matthew and Luke had Mark's gospel before them as they composed their own. They used much of Mark's gospel, while adding many stories (e.g. the birth accounts) and rearranging some of Mark's material. Thus these three gospels look alike ("synoptic" = "seeing together").

On the other hand, although John is similar to the first three gospels in his account of the Passion, he has very little in common with the rest of the other gospels. This makes it quite clear that John did not depend on them as he wrote his gospel. He is *not* a "look-alike" gospel.

4. For a definition of fundamentalism, please refer to p.19. A possible example:

> Everyone knows that the English word "let" means "to allow, to permit" something. A long time ago, it meant just the opposite, "to hinder." If someone refuses to admit that fact, he will never understand why a ball that hits the net in a tennis game is called a "let ball."

5. People often *selectively listen for* what they want to hear rather than *honestly listen to* what someone is really saying. Surely many

real-life examples of such "selective listening" could surface in a discussion of this point. (Cf. p.19 for a simple articulation of this basic biblical principle.)
6. (Cf. pp.15-17) In the long line crowding past DaVinci's *Mona Lisa* at the Louvre in Paris, a woman was heard to say to her husband: "Wasn't that beautiful?" (=Pre-critical). Meanwhile, a young man sat on the cement bench some ten yards away. He was simply gazing at the painting, occasionally smiling and turning the pages of DaVinci's biography. He had been there for two hours, and would probably be there until the museum closed (=Critical and Post-critical observor).

Concerning assignment and discussion questions for Chapter 2 (pp.37-38):

To begin with, ask: when and where did each person read the whole gospel? was it easy to find the time and quiet to do so? had they ever done this before, in one sitting? what was the most rewarding/most problematic aspect of their reading the whole gospel?

Then elicit from them their reflections on the overriding purpose Mark had as he sat down to write his gospel (Step 1); i.e., his desire to explain that his Christians were suffering and confused about their plight because they did not understand that being a follower of Jesus Christ meant following him to the cross as well as to resurrection glory.

Some hints or direction that will be helpful in discussing the questions under DURING THE READING:

Jesus emerges as a powerful but misunderstood person every time he cures someone and tells the cured person *not* to talk about it; they always disobey him and spread the news of their cure, causing people to think that Jesus is a political savior whose only purpose is to alleviate all pain from life. Examples: 1:40-45, 5:1-20, 7:31-37.

The disciples, especially Peter, are characterized as blind and rather dulled to the many hints that Jesus gives to them about his mission and destiny. Examples: 6:4-6, 6:49-52, 8:14-21, 8:31-33, 9:30-32, 14:32-42, 14:66-72, 16:8.

Jesus' humanity stands out in the following sections, because he is presented as one who expresses many human emotions and because he is so misunderstood by those around him. Examples: 1:41 and 2:16f., 3:21, 4:38, 5:43, 6:34, 7:24-30, 10:13-15, 11:12-14, and 15:34.

The climax of 8:27-38 follows upon all

the miraculous deeds of Jesus. Are his disciples ready to follow him on his way? The climax of 16:1-8 proves that he has been raised from the dead. Not even the angel's message stirs the women to announce the good news. Did anyone really believe in Jesus' true identity as Suffering and Risen Son of God? Do we?

Some hints or direction that might be helpful in discussing the questions under AFTER THE READING:

> Jesus seems a little intolerant in Mark's gospel. He even gets angry at times. Yet real faith demands that we accept Jesus as he is, and as he lives and dies, not as we want him to be! Mark's portrait of Jesus, so relegated to the shadows for centuries, is not the comfortable picture of "gentle Jesus" that many of us grew up with.

> Some passages that describe who a follower of Jesus is: 8:34-37, all of chapter 10, 13:32-37.

> Some passages that summarize who Jesus is: 3:31-35, 8:27-33, 10:32-45.

*Concerning assignment and discussion
  questions for Chapter 3* (p.50):

In your comparative study of Mark 8:27-34, Matthew 16:13-23, and Luke 9:18-22, did you discover the following major differences:

1. That Matthew has added three very significant verses (Mt 16:17-19) about Peter, the one to whom Jesus gives the keys of the kingdom?
2. That Luke has omitted the two significant verses found in Mark (8:32-33) and in Matthew (16:22-23) which describe Jesus' displeasure with Peter?

Both of these major differences will be seen again in the chapter that deals with this (i.e., Chapter 4).

*Concerning assignment and discussion
  questions for Chapter 4* (pp.58-60):

Concerning SECOND DAY: MIRACLES.

> There are only three miracle stories found in cc. 9-16, in contrast to eighteen miracle stories in cc. 1-8. These few miracles have a special emphasis to them:

a) the possessed boy in c. 9:14-29

Jesus cures the boy, *only after* the disciples couldn't. The emphatic point of this story is *aimed at those who wish to follow* Jesus: you lack trust in God (v.19) and neglect prayer in your desire to follow me (v.29). Attention, followers of Jesus!

b) the blind man in c.10:46-52

This miracle story will be treated in more detail in the next chapter. Briefly, this blind man believed in Jesus and *followed him up the road to Jerusalem* (v.52). The road leads to the cross and to death. How many "followers of Jesus" follow him there with their eyes wide open?

c) the resurrection in c.16:1-8

The women were the only followers of Jesus who were present at the cross and at the empty tomb. But even they disobey the angel who tells them to inform Jesus' disciples and Peter about the resurrection (v.7). They leave the tomb afraid, and say nothing to anyone. Are we afraid to spread the good news about Christ's *resurrection and cross*?

Concerning SECOND DAY: TEACHINGS.

Jesus is "teacher" in cc. 1-8 a few times. For example, in c.1:15, 1:21, and 1:39,

Jesus says the kingdom of God is at hand—yes, he taught with authority, but *what* did he teach?

He taught about forgiveness of sin, fasting, and the Sabbath (in c. 2), about the devil (in c. 3), and about the kingdom of God in parables (in c.4). But in each of these situations, no one seems to understand what he is getting at. Not even the disciples. ("You don't understand?" 4:13 . . . "He kept explaining things privately to his disciples" 4:34).

Mark realizes that Jesus' most important teachings (which appear in cc. 8-10) can only be understood in the light of the primary teaching about the cross (8:31-33, 9:30-32, and 10:32-34).

Below you will find some REALIZATIONS AND RESOLUTIONS of others who have prayerfully studied this section of Mark's gospel (Mk 8:27-38).

"I like to be comfortable. I like to feel the joy, peace, consolation of the resurrection. But the risen Lord is the crucified One too. It is only through the mystery of the cross that we experience the resurrection. To share Jesus' life is to share in his suffering and death . . . I find this call, this challenge, frightening. It means I cannot be content in my own little world; I cannot go about life according to my own plans. I have to open myself in love. When it hurts to love, I am called to love more. It also means that suffering will always be a part of my life. But suffering is not an end in itself; it is redemptive because it is participation in the cross of Christ and it leads to life . . . Jesus, teach me to respond openly to the mystery of suffering in my own life; for it is through suffering and death to self that I will live with you."

"The response that this section elicits from me is *commitment*. Just as the apostles avoided making a commitment to Jesus by any open recognition of him as the Christ who had to die, so also do I have to respond to *Christ's way* if I truly recognize him as the Christ. This means I must expect suffering in this life and must, in some way, unite that suffering with the suffering of Christ."

"This passage has many applications today for me, for the Church, for everybody. It is always tempting to compromise and take the easy way out of things . . . water down

Christ's message with just enough human wisdom to make it palatable. I can see myself doing that. I can see the Church doing it. Until I and the Church as a whole see value in suffering and see our union with Christ in it, I wonder if we can say we are following Jesus' way. This is a difficult question, and one that I think about a lot. God, give me strength to follow your way."

"Just like the apostles, we too must realize that the "Messiah" has something to do with us. If we believe deeply that Jesus is the Messiah, and if we too wish to follow him, then very seriously, we too *must* take up our cross daily. This is not just an intellectual affirmation; it can't be! It must be a lived faith. We must deny ourselves and follow."

"Jerusalem is now my home town. There is a cross with my name written on it; a road with plenty of room. In 8:34 Jesus asks the *crowd* to come and listen. That's *me*. Honestly, how real is suffering in my life? Do I accept it when it comes, or do I have to go out and look for it so I can say "all right . . . now I've suffered today." How do I prove my discipleship? Well, I *do* give up the pro football game some Sundays. Hold on! How about the guy who just wants to talk, to clear his head? The one who comes knocking at my door when I'm all set to do something? Self denial? Would I really die for him?"

"Mark speaks to me in this passage. More than that, Christ himself speaks to me personally now. He asks if I'm ready to stick with him all the way. Anxious to say yes, yet hesitant to give up all, I stand at this point with my eyes and ears more open to him now than ever before. I hope my *yes* will be more articulated very soon. I'm ready to join the "losing" team . . . rather than be a "spectator" any longer."

Concerning assignment and discussion questions for Chapter 5 (pp.69-71):

Concerning THIRD DAY

On the question of divorce and remarriage:

a) Major difference: Mark and Matthew both give the Lord's teaching on marriage and divorce. But Matthew inserts the phrase "except for unchastity" (in Mt 19:9, after "whoever divorces his wife and marries another commits adultery"). Mark does not have that phrase.

b) The "exception clause" inserted into Jesus' teaching by Matthew seems to "soften" Jesus' command. It is commonly thought that the "exception" referred to is some illegal sexual union which in Matthew's eyes was not a marriage in the first place. Thus people in such illegal unions could break them, and this strengthens the force of the prohibition of divorce and remarriage rather than weakening it.

c) The major message common to both is that divorce and remarriage is forbidden by the Lord. And no Jewish teacher had, up to that time, ever dared to formulate as God's will what Jesus does so forcefully: "Whoever divorces his wife and marries another, commits adultery" (Mk 10:11 and Mt 19:9).

d) The difficult teaching of Jesus comes clearly through the texts of Mark and Matthew: *no divorce and remarriage.* What does the Church teach today? Are there any marriages, even in Catholic ceremonies, that are not really valid? Should not we all become better informed about the slow but solid development in the Church's understanding of God's will about marriage?

On the question of riches:

> a) Two major differences appear in these sections of Mark and Matthew about riches: 1) Mark says that Jesus told the rich man "to go, sell what you have and give to the poor, and you will have treasure in heaven; and come, follow me" (Mk 10:21). Matthew says: *"If you want to be perfect*, go, sell, etc." (Mt 19:21). Thus, to be a follower of Jesus in Mark's gospel, you have to give up *all* and follow; whereas, in Matthew's gospel, you give up all, *if you want to be perfect.* 2) At the end of the section, Matthew's Jesus promises that those who give up all things for his sake will "receive a hundred-fold, and inherit eternal life" (Mt 19:29). Mark spells this out: "there is no one who has left all that will not receive a hundred-fold now in this time, houses and brothers and sisters and mothers and children and lands, and *persecution besides*, and in the age to come eternal life" (Mk 10:30).
>
> b) Since Matthew wrote *after* Mark, he has changed Mark's rendition of Jesus' teaching, and seems to "soften" the call to discipleship. In Matthew's gospel, it seems like there can be some disciples who do not give up all to follow Jesus . . .

only the perfect need do that (Mt 19:21). And Mark makes it clear that the Christian will be rewarded here in this life for giving up all to follow Jesus . . . yes, you will get a hundred-fold of what you give up, and *much suffering too!*

c) Both Mark and Matthew are encouraging their hearers to become detached from money and possessions. There can be no true attachment to Jesus if we are grasping to our possessions.

d) Where does our security lie? In him alone? Do I seek first the kingdom of God and the way of the Lord? Or am I constantly distracted and drawn to material security and success? Am I a perfect follower (according to Matthew 10:21)? Am I a follower of Jesus at all (according to Mark 10:21)?

Concerning FIFTH DAY

The Bible is God's Word for man, communicated through inspired authors like Mark, Matthew, Luke, John, and Paul. Even *within* the Bible we see the development of how the Church came to understand God's will in certain issues, like detachment from riches. (Recall the change in Matthew concerning riches, just ten years after Mark wrote!) As the Church attempts to interpret God's will for man, she is guided by the Holy Spirit much as inspired authors were. Consequently, Church tradition and the Church's development of doctrine over the ages is merely a continuation of what God did in his own Word. Do we believe the Spirit is still at work in the Church today, as it was in the lst century?